MiG-21
Cold War Warrior

Front cover illustration: A formation flight of Polish MiG-21PFMs. The 'Fishbed' is in operational service in all WarPac countries and is still the backbone of all the Soviet Union's satellite countries' air forces.

Back cover illustrations: Top, MiG-21PF of the Luftstreitkrafte der Nationalen Volksarmee high over the German Democratic Republic. Both aircraft are equipped with AA-2 'Atoll' dummy barrels, which record if the 'target' has been destroyed or not. **Below,** Polish pilots return from a mission in their MiG-21MFs. The life-jacket is carried on all operations near or over the Baltic Sea.

1. Natural metal MiG-21R armed with two K-13A AA-2 'Atoll' missiles. Although this is a reconnaissance variant, the centre-line recce pod is missing. The RWR pod on the wingtip clearly denotes the MiG-21R. The MiG-21 'Fishbed' is the most widely produced modern fighter in the world and serves with many nations in Europe, Central America, Asia and Africa. [*Lech Zielaskowski*]

MiG-21
Cold War Warrior

HANS-HEIRI STAPFER

ARMS AND
ARMOUR

▲2

Arms and Armour Press
A Cassell Imprint
Villiers House, 41–47 Strand,
London WC2N 5JE.

Distributed in the USA by
Sterling Publishing Co. Inc., 387
Park Avenue South, New York,
NY 10016-8810.

Distributed in Australia by
Capricorn Link (Australia) Pty.
Ltd, P.O. Box 665, Lane Cove,
New South Wales 2066.

Designed and edited by DAG
Publications Ltd. Designed by
David Gibbons; edited by David
Dorrell; layout by Anthony A.
Evans; typeset by Ronset Type-
setters Ltd, Darwen, Lancashire;
camerawork by M&E Reproduc-
tions, North Fambridge, Essex;
printed and bound in Great
Britain by The Alden Press,
Oxford.

British Library Cataloguing in
Publication Data
Stapfer, Hans-Heiri
MiG-21.
1. MiG-21 aeroplanes
I. Title
623.7463
ISBN 1-85409-039-9

2. MiG-21PF in flight over
the countryside. This fighter
is unarmed but carries
K-13A missile rails to accommodate AA-2 'Atoll' mis-
siles. [*Lech Zielaskowski*]

INTRODUCTION

The Soviet-designed Mikoyan Gurevich MiG-21 delta-winged fighter is still, numerically, the world's most produced modern fighter. This outstanding aircraft has been widely exported and remains the backbone of all Warsaw Pact air forces. The fighter saw action in the Middle East in the war with Israel, and proved itself a fine combat aircraft over the jungles of Vietnam. It was used by the Iraqi Air Force in the war against Iran and is still in active combat service in Afghanistan, where pilots of the Soviet-sponsored Kabul regime fly daily missions against the rebels in their civil war. On the other side of the globe the MiG-21 is used by the Nicaraguan Air Force against American-sponsored rebels.

More than thirty years after its maiden flight, the MiG-21 is still regarded as a reliable and modern weapon. The long operational life of the type has been made possible by progressive development over the years. The ultimate production variant, the MiG-21bis-SAU, has very little in common with the original MiG-21F. Modern MiG-21s have more sophisticated electronics and can carry a greater weapons load a longer distance, but they are no longer the nimble combat aircraft with outstanding flight characteristics that they once were. This is especially true when fully loaded with three 490-litre drop tanks and fully armed; the MiG-21 then is as nimble as a cow and quite tricky to fly.

The roots of the MiG-21 go back to the mid-1950s, straight into the Cold War period between East and West. On each side of the Iron Curtain engineers and designers developed new weapons to face the threat from the 'other side'. The MiG-21 was designed in response to a requirement for a Mach 2 fighter to replace the MiG-19 'Farmer'.

Initially, the MiG design bureau developed a swept-wing fighter with a single Mikulin TRD-9E engine. The first prototype, designated Ye-2, flew for the first time on 14 February 1955 with test pilot G. Mossolov at the controls. Further swept-wing experimental aircraft followed: the Ye-2A with a more powerful RD-11 engine, and the Ye-50 with an additional Type S-155 rocket engine.

The delta wing came about a year later in reality. Similar to the swept-wing fighter, a considerable amount of research on the best wing configuration had been made by specialists at the TsAGI (Central Aerodynamics and Hydrodynamics Research Institute). By that time the new Mach 2 fighter was still under evaluation and the first delta-winged experimental aircraft, the Ye-4, was built in 1955 and 1956. On 16 June 1956 the test pilot G. Sjedov took the Ye-4 for its first flight. The Ye-4 was soon followed by the Ye-5. The Ye-6 prototype was the basic variant for the first production version of the new Mach 2 fighter, the MiG-21F.

NATO allocated the ASCC-Reporting name 'Fishbed' to the MiG-21. The first thirty MiG-21Fs were produced in 1958. There were sixteen sub-variants built of this first mass production type. They were produced in two plants at Moscow and Tbilisi. Numerically the most important sub-variant was the MiG-21F-13. All WarPac countries were equipped with the MiG-21F-13 and Finland became the first non-communist country to receive the MiG-21F-13 in 1963.

Series production of the next variant started in 1962. This was the MiG-21PF which had an enlarged nose to accommodate the RP-21M 'Saphir' radar. All internal armament was deleted and the sole armament consisted of either AA-1 'Alkali' or AA-2 'Atoll' air-to-air missiles. The MiG-21PF followed the MiG-21FL with an enlarged tail and the MiG-21PFM with a new two-piece canopy and the new KM-1 ejection seat. MiG-21PFs specially modified for high altitude were designated MiG-21PFV. As the Israeli and Vietnam wars clearly showed, some form of internal armament was necessary – rather like 'life insurance' for the pilot. To solve this problem a GP-9 gunpod was fitted on the centre-line under the fuselage. These aircraft were called MiG-21SPS-K or MiG-21PFMA. A neat new feature on the MiG-21PFM and subsequent variants were blown flaps. These SPS flaps bled very hot high-pressure air from the main engine and blasted it at supersonic speed in a thin sheet over the top of the flaps. This stabilized the aircraft when on final approach and lowered the landing speed.

The MiG-21S became the first type of the third generation of 'Fishbed'. All aircraft in this series had an enlarged dorsal spine, a more powerful engine and improved fuel capacity. The MiG-21S followed the MiG-21M, which had a centre-line-mounted GSh-23L cannon with 220 rounds which were wrapped around the fuselage between the skinning and the engine air intake duct. The MiG-21M also had an angle of attack transmitter on the nose on the port side. The MiG-21M was followed by the MiG-21MF and MiG-21SM. The two reconnaissance variants of the fighter, the MiG-21R and MiG-21RF, lacked armament but carried a large recce pod on the centre-line pylon instead, as well as RWR-pods on the wing tips.

The first variant of the fourth generation was the MiG-21SMT. Extensive use of titanium resulted in a considerable weight reduction. The fourth generation MiG-21s had much improved avionics and a better cockpit layout. The MiG-21SMT differed from the MiG-21MF and MiG-21SM in having a swollen dorsal spine which accommodated a large fuel tank. The MiG-21SMT was produced only in limited numbers and was not exported outside the Soviet Union.

The MiG-21bis became the ultimate production variant of the 'Fishbed'. Compared with the MiG-21MF, it had a dorsal spine extension which led more into the tail fin. The new R-25-300 powerplant gave improved performance. The MiG-21bis had so little in common with the first production variant of the 'Fishbed' that the suffix 'bis' (from the French for 'again' or 'twice') was more than appropriate.

In addition to the fighter, the MiG design bureau also developed a two-seat trainer version. The first trainer reached the training units as the MiG-21U. Externally almost untouched, the trainers were progressively upgraded in parallel with the fighters. The MiG-21US was a version of the MiG-21PFM and also had the SPS blown flaps. The ultimate trainer variant, the MiG-21UM, is the companion of the third-generation fighter, the MiG-21MF. This variant is equipped with a periscope on top of the instructor's canopy to improve the hitherto poor forward view.

The MiG-21 is still in operational service in vast numbers with many air forces all over the world. It is unlikely that all these aircraft will be replaced before the beginning of the next century. Without doubt the MiG-21 is the most successful design to emanate from the Mikoyan and Gurevich design bureau and it is most unlikely that this success, either in numbers produced or length of operational lifetime, will be eclipsed by any other design from the MiG bureau in the future!

▲3 ▼4

3. The first MiG-21 prototype was the Ye-2, which first flew on 14 February 1955 with G. Mossolov at the controls. In contrast to the Ye-2A, it lacked wing fences and national markings on the upper wing surfaces.

4. The first prototypes were built with a swept wing, such as the Ye-2A, which was first flown by Grigorji Sjedov and attained a speed of Mach 1.78. This was the second prototype variant and was powered by an RD-11 engine of 5,100kg thrust. Even at this early stage of development armament was carried. The first delta-winged prototype flew more than two years after the first swept-wing prototype, but flight trials clearly showed the advances of the delta-wing fighter and the swept-wing project was phased out. The Ye-2A was built in 1955 and flown in competition with the delta-winged Ye-4. [Robert Gretzyngier]

5. Swept-wing prototype Ye-2A with the new RD-11 engine installed. The earlier Ye-2 was powered by a TRD-9E.

5▲ 6▼

6. Ye-2A during trials. It was the swept-wing competitor of the delta-wing Ye-4. It had a similar overall appearance to the MiG-21, but the engine tailpipe and undercarriage were completely different.

7▼

7. The Ye-5 prototype was the second delta-winged prototype built. Armed with three NR-30 cannon, the Ye-5 was completed in 1956 and first flown by Vladimir Nefjedov. The Ye-5 can be considered as the pre-prototype for the first production variant, the MiG-21F. [*Robert Gretzyngier*]

8. The Ye-6 prototype was similar to the early production MiG-21F. It first flew in 1958, was powered by an R-11 F-300, and was armed with two NR-30 cannon.

▲8 ▼9

9. Pilots scramble to their MiG-21Fs. The first production machines were delivered in 1958 and had the small tail fin, which was later enlarged. They had an armament of two NR-30 cannon and could each carry a K-5 (NATO AA-1 'Alkali') air-to-air missile. The national marking is natural silver with a small red outline.

10. Czech Air Force MiG-21F-13 'Black 1114' after touch-down at Prerov. The pilot uses both airbrakes and the white brake chute. The Czech-built MiG-21F-13s were produced by Aero Vodchody. Initially the Czechs used the designation S-106 for the MiG-21 ('S' for Stihacka/Fighter) but later dropped it in favour of the original Soviet designation.

▼10

11. MiG-21F-13 'Black 0312' landing at Prerov with both airbrakes fully deployed. Note that part of the NR-30 cannon fairing is also a part of the airbrake. The dark area around the NR-30 muzzle is the blast shield of heavy steel, necessary since the blast of the cannon could damage the thin alloy skin.

12. Czech MiG-21F-13 '0608' deploys its brake chute on landing. The first variants carried the brake chute in a container on the port side of the tail. Unlike Soviet machines, the Czech-built MiG-21F-13s had a nonglazed section behind the canopy. About 200 of these fighters were produced in Czechoslovakia.

▲13

13. MiG-21F-13 'Black 0607' is prepared for a sortie at Prerov Air Base, the training centre for pilots. A ground crewman has taken away the steps from another aircraft. All the canopies on the MiG-21F variants were of one piece and opened to the front. Ground crew wear white helmets with in-built ear protection. The F-13s were fitted with the first generation of ejector seats, the SK-1, which permitted a safe ejection up to a speed of 400km/h and from a height of at least 150 metres above ground.

14. MiG-21F-13 'Black 0312' undergoing an engine check. Portable protective netting has been placed in front of the air intake to prevent foreign debris entering the engine. The dorsal spine covering has been removed and the various pipes and fuel lines are checked with instruments. A number of other panels on the tail fin and fuselage have been removed for proper checking too. Usually when an aircraft is maintained, canvas is put on the wing to avoid damage by the ground crew's shoes.

▼14

15. MiG-21F-13 (right) and MiG-21U trainer on the ramp. The MiG-21F-13 is equipped with a Syrena 2 tail radar warner, installed above the rudder. The three-pole antenna belongs to the Chrom Nikiel IFF system, better known to NATO as 'Odd Rods'. The first half of the ventral fin is bright olive green, the same colour as the air intake cone. The antennae on the wing tip belong to the RV-UM radio altimeter, which operates up to an altitude of 1,200 metres.

16. Polish groundcrew work on a 'contaminated' MiG-21F-13 during an exercise; they are wearing L-2 chemical protection dress. These aircraft carry the small inboard flaps which were typical on all 'Fish-beds' before the SPS-blown flaps were introduced. The first Polish MiG-21F-13s were allocated to the famous 1st Fighter Regiment, which was born in battle during the Second World War. It was in 1944 that the pilots of the 1st Polish Fighter Regiment flew their first combat mission in Yakovlev Yak-1M fighters. The aircraft of the 'Warszawa' Regiment were first shown to the public on 12 September 1963.

15▲

16▼

▲17

▲18　▼19

17. MiG-21F-13 'Red 688' of the East German Air Force. The first aircraft of this type were allocated to Jagdfliegerergeschwader 8 (Fighter Regiment 8) 'Hermann Matern', and on 20 June 1962 the first German pilot in a MiG-21F-13 took off from East German soil. The Jagdfliegergeschwader 8 'Hermann Matern' is now equipped with the MiG-21MF and based at Marxwalde. The last MiG-21F-13s were withdrawn from operations in 1985, having served in the reconnaissance role with reconnaissance pods made in the German Democratic Republic.

18. Czech MiG-21F-13 '0310' taxi-ing towards the runway. While in the Soviet Air Force the tactical number usually consists of the last digits of the serial number, the meaning of the tactical number of Czech-built aircraft is different: the first two digits denote the batch and the last two the number of the aircraft built in that batch. Therefore 'Black 0310' was the tenth aircraft produced in the third batch. The number of aircraft built in each batch varies.

19. Line-up of MiG-21PFs during a winter exercise. All air intakes are protected by red coverings, each displaying the tactical number of the aircraft. The pitot boom has been moved from the bottom (MiG-21F-13) to the top on the MiG-21PF. The use of the RP-21M 'Saphir' radar in the centrebody made it necessary to enlarge the nose from 69cm (MiG-21F-13) to 91cm on the MiG-21PF. The aircraft nearest the camera has the tactical number 'Red 403' while the next machine carries tactical number 'Red 404'.

20. This pilot in his MiG-21PF is wearing the old VKK-4 flying suit which is also worn by MiG-19 and Sukhoi Su-7 pilots. The covering of the RD-21M radar screen can be seen. The screen provides the pilot with information on the distance, altitude and position of the object tracked. The screen can also give information as to whether the object tracked by the RD-21M radar is a friendly or enemy aircraft.

21. MiG-21PF 'Red 947' of the East German Air Force. It carries the 'Winged Q' symbol given to aircraft in good condition which have had a certain number of flying hours trouble-free. The aircraft is equipped with a twin launcher for AA-2 'Atoll' missiles. With these launching rails, four K-13A air-to-air missiles can be fired from a MiG-21PF. The first flight by a German pilot in a MiG-21PF was made on 17 August 1964 in the Soviet Union. The first flight of a MiG-21PF in East Germany was made on 10 December 1964 by a pilot of the 'Hermann Matern' Regiment, which is now based at Marxwalde.

▲22

22. A Polish pilot prepares for a mission. He is wearing the old VKK-4 dress and helmet. The KM-1 ejection seat has been introduced in the MiG-21PFM; all previous variants were equipped with the SK-1 seat. The KM-1 ejection seat is in light grey while the inside of the

▼23

cockpit and the canopy is painted in chromate green. The console on the starboard side holds the SOD-57M ATC transponder, whose functions include automatic response to secondary radars and a major enhancement of radar signature.

23. Line-up of Polish MiG-21PFMs. The nearest aircraft, 'Red 6602', is partially covered with canvas, while on the other machines the canopy is covered. Two of the hardstands are empty, indicating that these aircraft were on a mission. Coverings for the air intake and

jetpipe have been put away among the ground steps. The box is a generator to start the engines; it is also connected with a fuel pipeline. The trucks in the background are Star-660 with radio stations.

24. These two MiG-21PFs are equipped with K-13A missile rails and also carry a 490-litre drop tank on the centre-line fuselage pylon. On the MiG-21PF (also 'F and 'PFM variants) only a single fuel tank could be carried, the two wing pylons not being equipped as 'wet' pylons. The MiG-21F-13 has an internal fuel capacity of 2,280 litres plus 490-litre drop tank, making a total of 2,770 litres of fuel. [*Lech Zielaskowski*]

25. MiG-21PFM 'Red 01' using part of a motorway as the apron, while the other part of the motorway is used as a runway for take-off. The two-digit tactical number is quite unusual on Polish aircraft. The first exercise in landing and take-off from a motorway in Poland was made in 1972 by 'Fishbeds' of the 2nd Fighter Regiment 'Kraków'.

26. Mechanics check the engine tail nozzle of a MiG-21PFM. The covering around the nozzle has been removed to give better access. The MiG-21PFM uses the Tumansky R-11 F2S-300 with a thrust of 6,200kg. This engine was introduced into service in the late 1950s and was produced until about 1965. Compared with Western engines, the Tumansky is rather heavy and not so fuel-efficient. To carry more fuel automatically means less weapon load.

27. A MiG-21PFMA (SPS-K) with a GP-9 gunpod fitted on the centre-line, the only feature which differentiates it from the MiG-21PFM. Initially the MiG-21PF/PFM series were armed solely with air-to-air missiles, since it was thought that cannon armament was obsolete. However, combat experience in the Middle East and Vietnam showed that this was not so. Early air-to-air missiles tended to fail and it became evident that a fighter must be armed with cannon. The GP-9 gun pack was an interim solution for second-generation MiG-21s; the third generation was armed with the GSh-23L cannon. This MiG-21PFMA is also equipped with a UB-32 pod to accommodate 32 Type S-5 unguided hollow-charge missiles for ground-support duties.

28. Ground crew check the MiG-21PFM cockpit. The inside of the cockpit, including the canopy framing, is painted chromate green, while the instrument panel is painted black. The screen is the radar screen of the RP-21M 'Saphir' and on top is the ASP-PF-21 optical gunsight. This gunsight is used for the GP-9 gunpod (when fitted); it also functions on ground-support missions

▲26 ▼27

when Type S-5 unguided missiles are used, and it can be used to aim the various calibres of bombs which can be carried by the MiG-21. The red button on the left of the control stick is the emergency release button; if pressed, all external loads will be automatically released. The button on the right in black is for radio communication.

▼28

29. Two East German MiG-21PFMs scramble from a rainy runway during Exercise 'Soyuz 81' in late March 1981. The tactical number '560' on the first aircraft is in red. All East German aircraft carry tactical numbers which are never outlined. Both aircraft are equipped with R-60 rails to accommodate the AA-8 'Aphid' missile. The MiG-21 requires a take-off run of about 800 metres, depending on the weapon load and fuel carried. Both Luftstreitkräfte MiG-21PFMs are painted in well-worn light grey.

30. An East German MiG-21PFM, 'Red 758', takes off with the help of two SPRD-99 RATO rockets fitted under the rear fuselage. This natural-silver MiG-21PFM carries K-60 missile rails and the 'Winged Q' symbol. The 'Winged Q' is the East German equivalent of the Soviet 'aircraft in excellent condition' badge. The German Democratic Republic is the sole WarPac satellite country to decorate aircraft in good condition.

31. A Polish MiG-21PFM over typically Polish flat countryside. Unusually for a Polish MiG-21, 'Red 022' has the national marking applied to the rear fuselage. Together with Romania, Poland is believed to be the sole WarPac country to apply the national marking to the rear half of the fuselage. This 'Fishbed' is equipped with a 490-litre drop tank; after conversion it was possible to fit a 800-litre drop tank, but this was rarely used. The MiG-21PF/PFM has an internal fuel capacity of 2,580 litres, divided in six fuselage and four wing tanks, plus the centre-line fuselage drop tank, giving a total of 3,070 litres.

29▲

30▲ 31▼

32. The entire tail section of this MiG-21PFM can be removed to give better access to the engine and the control surfaces in the tail section. The PT-21UK chute container is open and the chute is not inserted. The large panel beside the national marking has also been removed and gives access to the N 12-51 booster and other equipment stowed in the tail fin. Part of the rear nozzle covering (made of steel due to the heat from the engine) has also been removed. The fairing between ventral fin and rudder is for the hydraulic pipe. The large fairing above the rudder is the tailplane crank fairing, followed by the cooling inlet.

33. MiG-21PFM 'Red 4915' touching down on a motorway emergency landing strip with airbrakes fully extended. The white smoke behind the aircraft is caused by the MiG-21's initial touch-down. The brake chute is not yet deployed. On this exercise this aircraft is equipped with two empty UB-16-57U pods. This Polish 'Fishbed' belongs to the 2nd Fighter Regiment 'Kraków'.

▲32　▼33

34. MiG-21PFM 'Blue 78' of the Soviet Air Force taking off from Domodedovo airfield in July 1967 with the help of two SPRD-99 RATO rockets. The pilot is about to retract the undercarriage. The SPRD-99 RATOs will be jettisoned after burn-out. The national markings have been applied to the upper surfaces of the wing. RATO is particularly useful for operation from airstrips damaged by enemy action and for starts from grass runways.

34▲

35. Line-up of East German MiG-21PFMs during Exercise 'Soyuz 81'. Some of the 'Fishbeds' are camouflaged, some not. 'Red 999' has the tactical number repeated on its drop tank. Interestingly, on the PWD-5 pitot tube the same number should be repeated, but there the number '5810' is inscribed in red. The arrow for the ejection seat release is in yellow and the inscription 'Rettung Drücken' is in black.

35▲ 36▼

36. Formation of natural-silver MiG-21PFMs of the East German Air Force. By this time the national marking had also been applied to the upper surfaces of the wing. All three aircraft are equipped with K-60 rails to accommodate the AA-8 'Aphid' air-to-air missile. The two 'Fishbeds' behind the leading aircraft, 'Red 17043', have their airbrakes extended to hold formation. By now all MiG-21PFMs in service with the East German Air Force are painted either light grey or camouflaged in brown earth and olive drab.

37. Ground crew check the Type PWD-5 pitot boom on a MiG-21PFM; two connection wires lead from the front of the probe to the check instrument. A third man sits in the cockpit to check the various instruments. The antenna in front of the nosewheel bay is the Chrom-Nikiel IFF. The nosewheel bay and the inside of the nosewheel doors are painted in chromate green while the conical centre-body is painted bright olive green.

38. Two Polish MiG-21PFMs prepare to taxi on to a motorway for take-off. No national markings have been applied to the upper surfaces of the wing, but there is an additional national insigna on the rear half of the fuselage. Both aircraft have SPS blown flaps, which reduce landing speed and improve yaw stability on landing.

39. Flight line of Polish MiG-21PFMs. The 'Midget' trainer in the foreground is a Polish-built SBLim-2, a trainer which has been converted from a MiG-15bis airframe. 'Red 1305' is a MiG-17F. Both the MiG-15UTI (SBLim-2) and MiG-17 are used as trainers in MiG-21 units. Some of the MiG-21PFMs have the SOD-57M transponder filter aerial painted in bright olive green; some are silver. The function of the SOD-57M transponder on top of the tail fin is to enhance the radar signature for the ground radar.

40. Two MiG-21PFM pilots with VKK-6 flying suits discuss a mission on the map. As standard, the inside of the canopy of MiG-21PFM 'Red 7814' is painted in chromate green, as is the console behind the front windscreen. The clear squared part of the pilot's

▲37 ▼38

trousers can accommodate a map or vital information on a mission.

41. Line-up of MiG-21PFMs with a Polikarpov Po-2 in front gives an impression of the size difference between a Second World War aircraft and a modern fighter. The Po-2 biplane was highly successful as a night 'nuisance' bomber; pilots often shut off the engine and glided it to the target, mainly German troop concentrations, in complete silence. Such attacks caused havoc to the morale of German soldiers on the Eastern Front. Placing a Po-2 in front of a MiG-21 'Fishbed' is not as strange as one might expect. The Polish 2nd Fighter Regiment 'Kraków' was formed in the Soviet Union as a night bomber regiment and flew the Po-2 alongside the Soviets in the 'Great Patriotic War'. Since the early 1960s this famous Polish unit has been equipped with the MiG-21 in various variants and still flies it today with MiG-21MFs from its base at Goleniów near the Baltic. [*Lech Zielaskowski*]

39▲

40▲ 41▼

42. In contrast to the early MiG-21F and 'PF versions, the MiG-21PFM has an enlarged tail fin without the fillet at the root. The MiG-21 is equipped with the KAP-2K autopilot. Several different settings are possible; the setting 'dumping' stabilizes the aircraft to the side, which is of help on landing; 'horizontal flight' is used when the pilot has lost his orientation and the aircraft automatically returns to a horizontal attitude. [*Lech Zielaskowski*]

▲42 ▼43

43. The MiG-21DPD was an experimental development for a STOL fighter using a converted MiG-21PFM fuselage. In a large bay in the fuselage two 3,500kg Koliesov ZM engines were installed. This additional lift gave the aircraft STOL capability but the MiG-21DPD was incapable of vertical or hovering flight. The MiG-21DPD remained a prototype and was not taken further. There is no tactical number allocated on the aircraft, just a badge of the test unit.

44. Two light-grey MiG-21Ms of the East German Air Force each with a 490-litre tank in silver. Tactical numbers '417' and '508' are, as usual, in red.

▼44

These two aircraft are returning from a mission in August 1979. The SPS blown flaps are in the down position. The rear-view mirror is missing and there is no gun blast panel below the inlet doors. The MiG-21M differed from the earlier MiG-21PF/PFM variants in having an enlarged dorsal spine and the lack of an antenna on the dorsal spine behind the cockpit.

45. Take-off of a Czech MiG-21M, 'Black 1114'. In the early stages the MiG-21M and MiG-21MF were operated without camouflage, but today most of the third-generation MiG-21 'Fishbeds' in the Czech Air Force are painted either light grey overall, or brown earth and olive drab. The third and fourth generations lost much of the agility and the nimble flight characteristics of the first MiG-21 variants.

46. Line-up of Polish MiG-21Ms (the two nearest aircraft) with some MiG-21 PFMs. The MiG-21M lacks the rear-view mirror which was fitted on all MiG-21MFs. At the beginning of its introduction, mixed formations of MiG-21Ms and MiG-21PFMs were quite common.

45▲ 46▼

▲47

47. MiG-21M of the Egyptian Air Force during Exercise 'Bright Star', which was a joint exercise involving Egyptian and American troops. This particular MiG-21M has been retrofitted with the TS-27AMSh rear-view mirror. The missing gun blast panel below the inlet blanking plate clearly denotes the MiG-21M version. The light-grey KM-1 ejection seat is rather worn and the air brake is extended. [*Dick Cole*]

48. An Egyptian MiG-21M during 'Bright Star'. Both airbrakes are fully extended and there is only one missile rail fitted on the inboard wing pylon. Egypt operated about 100 'Fishbeds' of various versions, but over the years they have been progressively upgraded with American avionics. On the left is a USAF KC-10 tanker and on the right a C-130 Hercules. [*Dick Cole*]

▼48

A. East German ground crew work on a MiG-21MF. One of the fuselage panels has been removed. The KT-92 mainwheel tyres have a diameter of 800 × 200mm.

B. An East German MiG-21MF – about to taxi out. The vehicle on the right is an Anlassgerätewagen AG-5 (starting device truck) built on an I.F.A. W-50 chassis.

▲C

C. MiG-21bis of the Magyar Légierö (Hungarian Air Force) flying over Budaörs airfield in June 1987. Hungarian MiG-21s carry four-digit numbers in red with a white outline. [*Urs Harnisch*]

D: A Romanian MiG-21 US on its hard stand. The Romanian Air Force operates about fifteen Mongol trainer aircraft; note the yellow-and-blue roundel within the red star, which indicates that the photograph was taken after the colour marking changes of 1985.

▼D

E: Engine check-up time for a MiG-21PF of the Romanian Air Force. The aircraft, 'Red 715', is held in place by two cables attached to the main undercarriage. The Roman-ians have fighter-interceptor regiments based at Grar-mata, near Timisoara, and Craiova.

F. MiG-21bis 'MG-130' at Kuopio-Rissala. The tail of the aircraft at the left be-longs to a BAe Hawk. Tradi-tionally Finland buys one-third of her weapons in the West, one-third in the Soviet Union and the last third comes from native pro-duction. Finland uses only the MiG-21F-13 and the MiG-21bis. [*Urs Harnisch*]

bombs. Primarily used in the air defence role, the MiG-21 can also be used as a ground-support aircraft, although the MiG-23BN 'Flogger-H' and the Sukhoi 'Fitter' series of aircraft are much better suited to the task.

H. Two East German MiG-21PFs on a practice mission over the German Democratic Republic. Each aircraft is armed with a single UB-16-57V pod for Type S-5 59mm unguided missiles. A '1' has been added in front of the true tactical number on both aircraft for this photographic session. The true tactical number on the aircraft in front is 'Red 951'; that of the 'Fishbed' in the background is 'Red 989'.

▲G
G. This picture shows the large variety of weapons that can be carried by a

▼H

Yugoslav MiG-21bis. 'Black 104' is painted light grey overall. Weapons from both

Soviet and Western manu-facturers are visible. The black bombs are 500kg

I. An unusual formation comprising an Egyptian Air Force MiG-21PFM alongside a USAF F-16 Fighting Falcon and an A-10 Thunderbolt during Exercise 'Bright Star' on 1 December 1981. Egypt's MiG-21s are equipped with a considerable amount of Western avionics.

J. East German MiG-21MF 'Red 86' at Holzdorf Air Force Base, 29 August 1985. The first digit of the tactical number has been over-painted. This aircraft is equipped with two UB-32 pods under each wing.

I ▲   J ▼

▲ K

K. A Yugoslav Air Force MiG-21bis, serial number 17125, the last three digits being repeated on the nose as the tactical number.

L. Soviet Air Force MiG-21bis 'Blue 05' on final approach to its home base. This aircraft is wearing only

▼ L

a two-tone camouflage of brown earth and olive drab. By now most of the MiG-21bis have been withdrawn from front-line Soviet regiments.

M. Finnish MiG-21F-13s on the ramp at Kuopio-Rissala. All the MiG-21s were allo-

cated to No 31 Squadron. 'MG-46' was delivered to Kuopio on 8 April 1963. The last MiG-21F-13s were withdrawn from service on 17 January 1986.

N. Even in the early 1990s, the MiG-21F-13 is still in active use with the Czech

Air Force. Some of the aircraft recently received a camouflage of two different shades of green, as well the four-digit tactical number outlined in white. Most of the few MiG-21F-13s now remaining are with the Advanced Training School at Kosice.

O. Recently the Polish Air Force began to adorn its aircraft with a unit badge as well as the crest of the city the aircraft are based at. This MiG-21MF, 'Red 7812', belongs to 41 Fighter Regiment based at Malbork and assigned to the Air Defence Command.

P. Polish MiG-21MF 'Red 7812' at Poznan Air Base, Summer 1989. Most of the Polish MiG-21MFs are now painted in an air-superiority grey. There are nine regiments with 35 aircraft each.

▲O ▼P

VARIANTS

MiG-21F (Version 72): First production variant with slim tail fin and two NR-30 cannon. No exports.

MiG-21F-13 (Version 74): Main production MiG-21F variant. In all there were 16 sub-variants of the 'F' version, which were built in two plants at Moscow and Tbilisi. Compared with the MiG-21F, the MiG-21F-13 had an enlarged tail fin and a single NR-30 cannon on the starboard side. Engine: R-11 F-300 developing 5,750kg thrust.

MiG-21PF (Version 76): Enlarged fuselage to accommodate the RP-21M 'Saphir'. Nose diameter increased from 69cm (MiG-21F-13) to 91 cm. Internal armament deleted. Two front airbrakes behind the nosewheel doors replaced the single airbrake on the MiG-21F. Fitted with KT-92 mainwheels of larger diameter than those on the MiG-21F. Engine: R-11 F2-300 of 5,950kg thrust.

MiG-21FL (Version 77): Enlarged tail fin without fillet as on MiG-21F/PF variants. Brake chute moved from a container on the port side of the tail to the PT-21UK brake chute container at the base of the rudder. Engine: R-11 F2-300 of 5,950kg thrust.

MiG 21PFV: Special variant of the MiG-21PF with improved ceiling performance for high altitude. The suffix letter 'V' stands for 'Visotny' (Altitude).

MiG-21DPD (Version 92): MiG-21PFM airframe converted to accommodate two 3,500kg-thrust Koliesov ZM engines in a bay in the fuselage. This gave the test aircraft STOL performance, but it was incapable of vertical or hovering flight. No production. Engine: R-11F2S-300 of 6,200kg thrust.

MiG-21PFM (Version 94): Two-piece canopy and KM-1 ejection seat which replaced the SK-1 seat used in previous variants. Introduced SPS flaps. Otherwise similar to the MiG-21FL (Version 77) Engine: R-11 F2S-300 of 6,200kg thrust.

MiG-21PFMA (SPS-K) (Version 94K): MiG-21PFM with GP-9 gun pod fitted on centre-line under the fuselage. The GP-9 pod housed a GSh-23 twin-barrel cannon and 200 rounds of ammunition. Apart from GP-9 pod, similar to MiG-21PFM (Version 94).

MiG-21S (Version 95): First third-generation MiG-21 with enlarged dorsal spine, but still with centrally mounted pitot tube and a single pylon under each wing. No internal armament carried. Engine: R-11 F2S-300 of 6,200kg thrust.

MiG-21M (Version 96): First third-generation MiG-21 to receive internal armament: a single GSh-23L cannon with 220 rounds of ammunition in the fuselage. The new PWD-7 pitot tube was offset to starboard. Angle of attack transmitter placed on the port side of the nose. The true MiG-21M lacked the Type TS-27 AMSh rear-view mirror, but some were later retrofitted. There were two wing pylons instead of one on previous 'Fishbed' versions. The outboard pylon is designed as a 'wet' point to carry a 490-litre drop tank. Engine: R-11F2S-300 of 6,200kg thrust; late batches R-11 F2SK-300.

MiG-21R (Version 94R): Reconnaissance variant with no armament, but RWR pod on each wingtip and large reconnaissance pod on centre-line fuselage pylon. Engine: R-11 F2S-300 of 6,200kg thrust.

MiG-21SM (Version 96): Improved variant of the MiG-21M. Production aircraft fitted with rear-view mirror, also gun-blast panel below the inlet blanking doors. Engine: R-13-300 of 6,600kg thrust.

MiG-21MF (Version 96): Similar to the MiG-21SM. Exported in large quantities to WarPac and other client states. Engine: R-13-300 of 6,600kg thrust.

MiG-21RF (Version 96R): Reconnaissance variant of the MiG-21MF. No armament, but RWR pod on wingtip and large reconnaissance pod on centre-line pylon. Engine: R-13-300 of 6,600kg thrust.

MiG-21SMT: Further development of the MiG-21SM. The 'T' denotes 'lightened' – titanium parts reduced weight. Externally distinguishable from the MiG-21SM/MF by the remarkably swollen dorsal spine, which housed an additional fuel tank. Engine: R-25-300 of 7,600kg thrust.

MiG-21bis: Featured considerable use of titanium components and new avionics. Compared with the MiG-21MF, the dorsal spine extends further into the tail fin. Considerably more fuel capacity than in previous variants. Engine: R-25-300 of 7,600kg thrust.

MiG-21U (Version 66-400): Developed from the MiG-21F-13. Two seats in redesigned nose section. No armament carried. Engine: R-11F-300 of 5,750kg thrust.

MiG-21U (Version 66-600): Trainer counterpart of the MiG-21PF, enlarged tail and chute container at base of the rudder. Engine: R-11F2-300 of 5,950kg thrust.

MiG-21US (Version 68): Counterpart of the MiG-21PFM. Equipped with SPS blown flaps. Antenna of the radio compass fitted on top of the instructor's cockpit. Engine: R-11F2S-300 of 6,200kg thrust.

MiG-21UM (Version 69): Counterpart of the MiG-21MF. Rear-view mirror placed on instructor's cockpit. Antenna placed on tail in front of the tail fin. Angle of attack transmitter fitted on port side of nose. KM-1U ejection seats replaced the SK-1 seats on MiG-21U/US. Engine: R-13-300 of 6,600kg thrust.

MiG-21I (ANALOG) (A-144): Development of the MiG-21MF to test the wing of the Tupolev Tu-144 supersonic airliner. It was fitted with a scaled-down wing of the Tu-144. The A-144 came too late in service to be of help in the Tu-144 programme but it served as a chase plane on the Tu-144's first flight on 31 December 1968. Engine: R-13-300 of 6,600kg thrust.

MiG-21F-13 ('FISHBED-C')

The MiG-21F-13 (Samoljot 74) was the main production variant of the E-6 Series. It was widely exported. On the MiG-21F-13 (Prototype designation E-6T) there was no port-side NR-30mm cannon; the early versions of the MiG-13 had two NR-30 cannon. Production of the MiG-21F-13 began with aircraft serial number 0815.

The MiG-21F-13 had the sensor boom on centre-line below the fuselage, a small dorsal spine, different main wheel doors and air brakes from other variants as well as only two pylons on each wing. It had a canopy that opened to the front and was of one piece.

CAMOUFLAGE

Silver Colour: Until the early 1970s all MIG-21s of various variants were delivered in natural metal finish. This practice was maintained in the Soviet Union and all WarPac countries.

Air-Superiority Grey: In the 1970s the Soviet Air Force and all WarPac countries began to paint interceptor MiG-21s (mainly the late variants MiG-21MF and MiG-21bis) in light grey overall, but this was not carried out thoroughly. There were frequently silver and light grey aircraft in use in the same regiment. When fresh, these aircraft were semi-matt, but after a time in service their finish came brighter.

Camouflaged MiG-21: In the 1970s the Soviet Union began to change its doctrine and decided that aircraft should be camouflaged since it was thought that the main part of combat missions flown would be at low altitudes. The camouflage applied depended on the area where the aircraft was used. In the European part of the Soviet Union the colours dark green, brown earth, light grey and olive drab were used. In the Asiatic part of the USSR machines were painted mainly olive drab and sand, with brown, grey and green added. Most of the MiG-21s are camouflaged in light blue, but light grey is also seen, although rarely.

MiG-21s in all areas of operations can be seen in either two-, three- or four-tone camouflage. In contrast to NATO which uses quite exact paint schemes, like 'European One', such standard schemes do not exist in the Soviet Air Force. It is simply directed that the upper surfaces should be camouflaged in various colours. As a result, each aircraft looks different from another. The camouflage also depends on what kind of paint is available and how old the paint is before it is applied. The painters have a great deal of freedom on how to paint an aircraft. When applied the paint is usually semi-matt, but becomes brighter with age and service.

COLOUR POINTS FOR THE MODELLER

Cockpit: Inside of cockpit is chromate green. Part of the instrumentation panel is black. KM-1 ejection seat is in light grey. Canopy framing is also chromate green inside.

Undercarriage: Silver but on late models it can also be light grey. Nosewheel and mainwheel bays on silver aircraft are mainly chromate green. The inside of the undercarriage covering plates can be either silver or chromate green – or on camouflaged aircraft, the same colour as the aircraft's undersurfaces.

Airbrakes: Insides of airbrakes are natural silver on aircraft without camouflage. On camouflaged aircraft the airbrake insides are painted in the same colour as the undersurfaces.

Conical centre-body: With very few exceptions the conical centre-body is painted in glossy olive green. It is painted the same colour as the SOD transponder filter aerial on the tail fin on most of the third- and fourth-generation MiG-21s.

Guided missiles: AA-2 'Atoll' and AA-8 'Aphid' are always painted white. The glossy IR head is black.

Unguided missiles: The UB-8, UB-16 and UB-32 pods were initially all natural silver, but some were repainted in light blue. Camouflaged MiG-21s carrying silver UB pods is quite possible.

Bombs: All bombs are painted dark grey. Stripes in different colours denote the purpose.

COLOUR OF NATIONAL MARKINGS AND TACTICAL NUMBERS

National Markings: Soviet national markings are, and have been since the later stages of the Second World War, large white with a small red outline. This is the standard national marking, but sometimes on silver aircraft the large white outline is not used and the bare silver of the skin is used instead. Until the mid-1970s the national markings were applied only to the tail fin and the undersurfaces of the wing, but the Soviets then also began to apply them to the upper surfaces of the wing. Most of the WarPac countries soon followed. Poland and Romania sometimes also paint the national markings on the tail fin and the rear part of the fuselage.

Tactical Numbers: In many cases the tactical number on the nose of the aircraft is the last two or three digits of the serial number; sometimes the first digits were taken instead, or none at all. Most Soviet units use two-digit tactical numbers, mainly red or blue numbers outlined in black on silver aircraft.

On camouflaged aircraft the tactical number is outlined in white. In some cases, only the white outlining is applied and painted against the camouflage, without painting the inside of the white outlined tactical number in another colour.

It should be noted that not all tactical numbers are white-outlined on camouflaged aircraft. It is believed that aircraft without outlined tactical numbers belong to the air defence units.

Special Markings: Special markings are rarely seen on MiG-21s although some have been painted for special occasions. Some aircraft carry the Guards symbol as a sign that this unit participated as a Guards Regiment during the 'Great Patriotic War' (World War Two). The most popular insignia is the *Otlitshnij Samoljot* badge, which shows that the aircraft is in perfect condition. It is a stencilled aircraft symbol and is usually applied in red.

ARMAMENT

MiG-21F-13/MiG-21PF

Guided Missiles: K-5 (RS-2US) – NATO designation AA-1 'Alkali'. This was the standard missile for the MiG-19 'Farmer'. It weighs 83kg and two can be carried on the wing pylons. This weapon was guided by a pencil beam sent out

MiG-21bis-SAU ('FISHBED-N')

The MiG-21bis and the MiG-21M series had two pylons on each wing, in contrast to the first MiG-21 variants, which only had one pylon per wing.

The MiG-21bis SAU was the ultimate production variant of the 'Fishbed'. Production of the MiG-21bis started in 1975 and lasted until 1983.

It had a dorsal spine leading deeper into the stabilizer as on the MiG-21MF; the MiG-21bis-SAU also received a centre-line antenna on the nose. In contrast to the first variants, the MiG-21bis had a rear-view mirror and the data boom fitted on top of the starboard side.

The MiG-21M and bis series had an angle-of-attack transmitter fitted on the portside on the front.

From MiG-21PFM onwards there was a parachute container on the base of the rudder. The horizontal stabilizer was also enlarged on the MiG-21PFM onwards.

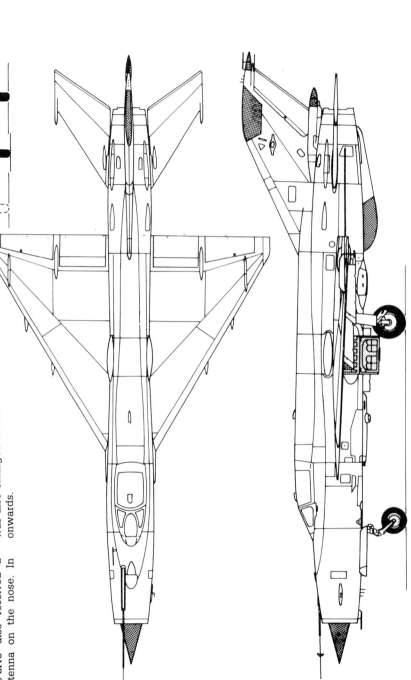

by the MiG-21's R2L radar. The pilot had to illuminate the target while the missile was on its way. Maximum range was 8km, but the preferable range was between 3,500 and 1,500 metres. A red light on the screen signalled when the MiG-21 had reached the safety belt of 2,000 metres. The K-5 could reach 1,650km/h and had a warhead which detonated just before impact.

K-13A – NATO designation AA-2 'Atoll' for infra-red variant. The K-13A was an exact copy of the American AIM-9B Sidewinder. About 50,000 were built and exported to some 26 client states. There are single and twin missile launching rails for the MiG-21 to accommodate either two or four K-13As. The AA-2 'Atoll' has a cruising speed of Mach 2.5 and a range of 3 to 4 miles.

Internal Armament (MiG-21F-13): The MiG-21F had two NR-30 cannon, while the MiG-21F-13 carried only a single NR-30 cannon with 60 rounds of ammunition on the starboard side. The Nudelmann-Richter NR-30 cannon was introduced to the Soviet inventory in 1954. It weighs 66kg and fires heavy 410gm rounds at a rate of 900 rounds per minute. It is a well tried and reliable weapon.

GP-9 Gun Pod (MiG-21PFMA): The GP-9 gun pod was fitted on the centre-line of the MiG-21PF or MiG-21PFM. The pod housed a GSh-23 twin-barrel cannon and 200 rounds of ammunition.

MiG-21MF/MiG-21bis

Guided Missiles: K-13A – NATO designation AA-2 'Atoll' with IR warhead; K-13A – NATO designation AA-2-2 'Advanced Atoll' with SARH (Semi-Active Radar Homing) head. This weapon has an increased length of 3.20m. The 'Advanced Atoll' is guided to the target by illuminating it with the 'Jay Bird' radar, which is installed in the MiG-21MF and MiG-21bis variants.

K-60 – NATO designation AA-8 'Aphid'. This small (2.15m long) missile is the new standard short-range missile in the WarPac inventory; it was first observed in 1976. It has a cruising speed of Mach 2.5 and a range of up to 5 kilometres. There is also a twin-launch rail in use, so with two R-60s on each pylon, theoretically up to eight AA-8s can be carried by a MiG-21 'Fishbed'.

Internal Armament (MiG-21MF/bis): All MiG-21s of the third and fourth generation are equipped with the GSh-23L twin-barrel cannon. This 23mm weapon has been developed on the basis of the Gast principle first employed in Germany in 1916. The recoil of one gun automatically loads and fires the other cannon. This results in an impressive rate of fire of 3,000 to 3,400 rounds per minute. The weapon itself weighs only 52kg. The ammunition is placed in the space between skinning and engine air duct and wrapped around the fuselage. Ammunition supply is about 220 rounds.

MiG-21 All Variants

Unguided Missiles: S-5 hollow-charge unguided missile.

This 57mm missile has been produced in vast numbers and widely exported. The S-5 missile weighs 38kg, has a warhead of 800gm and a length of 880mm. The missiles are fired from either UB-16-57U pods with 16 missiles or UB-32s with 32 missiles.

The early MiG-21F and MiG-21F-13 were also equipped initially with the UB-8 pod with eight S-5 missiles. The missile is mainly used for ground-support duties. Different warheads are available, such as high-explosive, fragmentation, etc.

S-24 missile. This is a large 240mm unguided missile with approximately the same dimensions as the K-13 'Atoll'. It is launched from the same type of rails as used for the AA-2 'Atoll' and AA-2-2 'Advanced Atoll'.

Bombs: All MiG-21 variants can carry bombs up to a weight of 500kg. Most common are the general-purpose bombs FAB 100, FAB 250 and FAB 500. If a 500kg bomb is carried on wing pylons, a small part of the mainwheel undercarriage covering plates has to be removed due to the diameter of the 500kg bomb. Stripes on the nose of the bombs denote the purpose; for example, two yellow stripes means high-explosive charge.

FUEL CAPACITY

MiG-21F-13: Internal, 2,280 litres in six fuselage and two wing tanks; external, 490 litres in single centre-line fuselage drop tank; total, 2,770 litres.

MiG-21PF/PFM: Internal, 2,580 litres in six fuselage (2,020 litres) and four wing tanks (560 litres); external, 490 litres in centre-line fuselage tank. Later there was a conversion to accommodate a 800-litre fuselage drop tank; total, 3,070 litres.

MiG-21MF: Internal, 2,600 litres in seven fuselage and four wing tanks; external, 1,470 litres in three 490-litre tanks on centre-line pylon and outboard wing pylons; total, 4,070 litres.

MiG-21bis: Internal 2,750 litres in seven fuselage and wing tanks. One large 470-litre tank in large dorsal spine; external, 1,470 litres in three 490-litre tanks on fuselage and wing pylons; total, 4,370 litres.

EJECTION SEATS

MiG-21F/MiG-21PF/MiG-21U/UM: The first- and second-generation MiG-21s were equipped with the Type SK ejection seat. This seat allowed a safe rescue up to speeds of 1,100km/h. To allow a safe ejection the aircraft had to have a speed of at least 400km/h and an altitude of 150m. All MiG-21s with the single-piece canopy which opened to the front were equipped with the SK-1 ejection seat.

MiG-21PFM/MF/bis/UM: All MiG-21s of the third and fourth generation, as well as the MiG-21UM trainer, were equipped with the KM-1 ejection seat. The designation 'KM' stands for 'krjeslo Mikoyan' (Seat Mikoyan). This seat assured a safe ejection up to a speed of 1,200km/h and an altitude of 25,000m. This is the nearest Soviet equivalent of a zero-zero seat, *but* for a safe ejection from the ground the aircraft must have a speed of at least 130km/h. The KM-1 includes two stabilization and one main chute. Incorporated in the KM-1 is an emergency oxygen supply (KP-27M) and a survival kit (NAS-7). The survival kit is connected to the pilot on a 15m-long wire. With the introduction of the KM-1 seat, the MiG-21 was produced with a two-piece canopy, which opens on the starboard side.

AVIONICS

MiG-21F-13

Airspeed indicator:	KUSI-2500K
Machmeter:	M-2, 5K
Compass:	KSI
Stiffness:	AGD-1
Automatic pilot:	KAP-2K
Radio (VHF):	R-802 (RSIU-5V)
Radio-compass:	ARK-10
Radio-altimeter:	RV-UM
Marker:	MRP-56P
ATC-transponder	SOD-57M
IFF:	Chrom-Nikiel (NATO 'Odd Rods')
Radar warner:	Syrena 2
Gunsight:	ASP-5ND
Radar rangefinder:	SRD-5M (NATO 'High Fix')

MiG-21PF/PFM

Radar:	RP-21M Saphir (NATO 'Spin Scan')
Gunsight:	ASP-PF-21
Automatic steering regulator:	ARU-3V
Stiffness:	DA-200
Voltmeter:	V-1
Manometer:	MV-12
Brake parachute on tail:	PT-21UK
Pitot tube:	PWD-5
Tail warner	Syrena 3M
Launch computer:	VRD-24
IR sight:	SIV-52

MiG-21M/MF

Pitot tube:	PWD-7
Autopilot:	AP-155
Two-pointer altimeter:	WDI-30K
Rear-view mirror:	TS-27AMSh
Radar:	'Jay Bird'

OPERATORS:

Afghanistan, Algeria, Angola, Bangladesh, Bulgaria, Cuba, Czechoslovakia, Egypt, Ethiopia, Finland, German Democratic Republic, Hungary, India, Indonesia, Iraq, Laos, Libya, Madagascar, Mongolia, Mozambique, Nicaragua, Nigeria, North Korea, North Yemen, Poland, Romania, Somalia, South Yemen, Soviet Union, Sudan, Syria, Uganda, United States of America, Vietnam, Yugoslavia, Zambia

TECHNICAL DATA OF MiG-21 VARIANTS

	Ye-5	MiG-21F	MiG-21F-13	MiG-21PFM	MiG-21MF	MiG-21bis	MiG-21U
Wingspan (metres)	7.40	7.15	7.15	7.15	7.15	7.15	7.15
Length (metres)	13.46	13.46	13.46	13.58	13.46	13.46	13.46
Height (metres)	4.10	4.10	4.10	4.12	4.12	4.12	4.12
Empty weight (kilogrammes)	4,800	4,900	4,871	5,100	6,000	5,350	4,900
Max T.O. weight (kilogrammes)	6,500	8,600	8,625	9,080	9,400	7,960	8,652
Powerplant	RD-11	R-11F-300	R-11F-300	R-11F2S-300	R-13F-300	R-25-300	R-11F-300
Thrust (kilogrammes)	5,000	5,750	5,750	6,200	6,600	7,600	5,750
Armament (Internal)	3 x NR-30	2 x NR-30	1 x NR-30	1 x GP-9	1 x GSh-23L	1 x GSh-23L	None
Number of pylons	None	2	2	2	4	4	2
Radar Type	SRD-5M	SRD-5M	SRD-5M	RP-21M	Jay Bird	Jay Bird	None
Max. speed (kilometres/hour)	2,000	2,125	2,125	2,175	2,230	2,230	2,125
Landing speed (kilometres/hour)	215	215	215	260	270	270	215
Service ceiling (metres)	18,000	19,000	19,000	19,000	19,000	19,000	19,500
Range (kilometres)	1,400	1,670	1,670	1,680	1,800	1,850	1,670
Crew	1	1	1	1	1	1	2
Internal fuel (litres)	2,280	2,280	2,280	2,580	2,600	2,750	2,280
Total fuel incl. drop tanks (litres)	2,280	2,770	2,770	3,070	4,070	4,530	2,770
Ejection Seat Type	SK-1	SK-1	SK-1	KM-1	KM-1	KM-1	SK-1

49. Overhaul of a Polish MiG-21R. It carries no national markings on the upper wing surfaces but the canvas on the wing should protect the skin from being damaged by the mechanics. The dorsal spine has been removed and gives a view of the various lines and pipes. There was no fuel tank in the dorsal spine of the MiG-21M and its subvariants; it was simply an aerodynamic feature. On the trolley the covering for the nozzle of the engine is visible.

49▲ 50▼

50. Polish MiG-21R 'Red 1423' prior to a mission. The large reconnaissance pod houses an AFA-39m camera and equipment to illuminate the area to be photographed if the mission is carried out at night. Most of the MiG-21Rs are equipped with a rear-view mirror, as on the MiG-21MF, but this particular 'Fishbed' lacks the TS-27AMSh mirror. Most MiG-21Rs carry two 490-litre fuel tanks on their outboard wing pylons.

51▼

51. This silver MiG-21R, 'Black 1921' of the Czechoslovak Air Force, has its air intake closed by the red covering, where the tactical number of the aircraft is repeated in white. It is quite a common practice to mark all the accessories belonging to an aircraft, including coverings on air intake and nozzle, to prevent unauthorized 'borrowing'. The pitot boom is also covered and connected with a wire to the air intake covering.

▲52

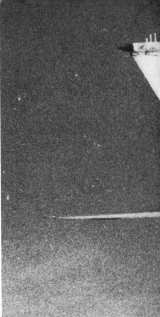

▲53 ▼54

52. MiG-21R 'Red 1911' on final approach. For a reconnaissance aircraft it carries a rather unusual load of two UB-16-57U pods for sixteen Type S-5 hollow-charge unguided missiles each, which are used on ground-support duties. This MiG-21R also lacks the rear-view mirror fitted to most reconnaissance aircraft. Due to the long range of the reconnaissance missions, the two 490-litre drop tanks are fitted on almost all MiG-21Rs.

53. Ground crew check the PWD-7 pitot boom of a Polish MiG-21R. In contrast to the MiG-21PF/PFM, the boom is offset to starboard. The panel for the electronic equipment is open. MiG-21s of the third and fourth generation have an angle of attack transmitter fitted on the nose. While the aircraft is on the ground, the transmitter is protected by a red covering to avoid damage. The trolley beside the nose-wheel is used to move the 'Fishbed' with the help of a truck.

54. Polish MiG-21R 'Red 1912' during a grim winter exercise. Air intake and tail pipe are covered, as well as

the canopy. The canvas on the fuselage can cover the entire machine to protect it against snow if parked outside a hangar. The poor soldier is probably dreaming about holidays in warmer places.

55. MiG-21R 'Red 1064' lacks the large reconnaissance pod on the centre-line fuselage, but the RWR pods on the wing tips denote this 'Fishbed' as a reconnaissance variant. They carry no internal armament, but the inboard pylon is fitted with AA-2 'Atoll' missile rails. [*Lech Zielaskowski*]

56. Viewed through the removed engine jet tail pipe of a MiG-21M, ground crew check a jacked-up MiG-21MF of the East German Air Force. A '1' has been painted in front of the true tactical number 'Red 513'. A device is fitted in front of the conical centre-body to calibrate the radar, as well as to check the pitot boom with instruments. This MiG-21MF belongs to Jagdfliegergeschwader 3 (Fighter Regiment 3) 'Wladimir Komarow' based at Preschen.

57. Ground crew handle a dark-grey 50kg practice bomb on the outboard wing pylon of a MiG-21MF. On the inboard wing pylon a silver UB-16-57U pod for sixteen Type S-5 hollow-charge missiles is fitted. An interesting feature of the main undercarriage doors of a MiG-21 is that, if a 500kg bomb is carried on the inboard pylon, the pointed part of the mainwheel undercarriage covering plate has to be removed due to the large dimensions of the 500kg bomb.

▲57 ▼58

58. Czech MiG-21MF 'Black 7714' about to touch down. Three 490-litre tanks are fitted on the outboard wing pylons and the centre-line fuselage pylon. The MiG-21MF has an internal fuel capacity of 2,600 litres which, with three 490-litre drop tanks, makes a total of 4,070 litres.

▼59

59. Engine check on light-grey MiG-21MF 'Black 4003' of the Czechoslovak Air Force. Note protective cage wheeled in front of the air intake to prevent debris ingestion by the R-13 F-300 engine. The rectangular hole in the front at the bottom of the cage is for use with the MiG-21F-13, whose pitot boom is fitted on the bottom of the nose. An instrument can be seen inserted in the dorsal spine to check fuel pressure and other data when the engine is running. The covering on the inlet blanking plate is necessary, since the airflow could easily capture a hand of the mechanic.

60. Another view of MiG-21MF 'Black 4003' during engine checks. Note the metal wire which leads from a hook in the ground to the main undercarriage. This is necessary to tether the aircraft since the brakes alone would be insufficient to hold it. The fire extinguisher is an important item – just in case . . .

61. Czech MiG-21MF 'Black 8207' camouflaged in brown earth and olive drab on the upper surfaces and light grey on the lower surfaces. The large white stripe around the rear half of the fuselage is an exercise marking. The R-60 missile rail is in silver.

▲62

62. MiG-21MF 'Black 9404' equipped with three 490-litre drop tanks painted olive drab on the upper surfaces and light grey underneath; interestingly, the cooling air inlet is still in silver. Flown in this configuration, the 'Fishbed' is as nimble as a cow, having lost the agility of the MiG-21F-13. Pilots consider that the MiG-21F-13 had the best handling characteristics, but during its development life

the type became increasingly heavy, a problem that could not be solved with increased power.

63. Take-off of MiG-21MF 'Red 578' boosted by two SPRD-99 rockets. Each inboard pylon has AA-8 'Aphid' rails, while the outboard has an AA-2 'Atoll' missile. It is believed that this aircraft belongs to Jagdfliegergeschwader 2 'Juri Gagarin' based at Trollen-

hagen in the north of the German Democratic Republic. This German unit is named in honour of the first man in space, who ironically, was killed aboard a MiG-15UTI. [*Harry Wisch via Air Force Monthly*]

64. It looks like a realistic scene on an airfield, but it is not. These aircraft are training objects for trainee mechanics at the Unteroffiziers-hochschule 'Harry

▲63

Kuhn' at Bad Düben in the German Democratic Republic. Bad Düben actually does not have a hard surfaced runway and all aircraft for this training unit have to be dismantled and taken there by truck. The trainees are clambering on a MiG-21MF, 'Red 529', whose pitot boom is covered by a black protective covering, while the air intake and the angle of attack transmitter on the nose are covered by red painted

▼64

65▲

coverings. The highly polished surface of 'Red 529' is not often seen on East German aircraft; most of them are semi-matt painted. The UB-16-57U pods are empty.

65. Overhaul of a MiG-21MF (foreground) and a MiG-21UM (background) in a hangar of Jagdfliegergeschwader 8 'Hermann Matern' at Marxwalde. Part of the fuselage is covered with canvas and some of the fuselage panels of both aircraft have been removed, as well as the covering of the nozzle. The tailplane crank fairing is removed. All the movable panels are painted chromate green on the inside. The reflecting light on the winglet is not clearly visible, but the national marking of the German Democratic Republic is also painted on the upper surfaces of the wing. The 'Hermann Matern' Regiment is the oldest MiG-21 'Fishbed' operator, having received its first MiG-21F-13s in 1962.

66. Stabsfeldwebel Klaus Jäckel inserts the brakechute in its container at the base of the rudder using the pilot's steps. Note the fuel pipeline under the tail and the bottle with the wires on it. This bottle is to collect the fuel from the engine bay. This is a light-grey overall MiG-21MF, while the MiG-21MF on the left has an unusual camouflage of medium green and light brown. This version of the MiG is equipped with 'Jay Bird' radar and can therefore carry the AA-2-2 'Advanced Atoll' with semi-active radar-homing head.

66▼

▲67

67. A Mil Mi-6A 'Hook' helicopter demonstrates its lift capability with a MiG-21MF, 'Red 2010', as underslung cargo. The Mi-6A, SP-ITA, belonged to the Polish heavy lift company INSTAL, whose three 'Hooks' have since been transferred to the Polish Air Force and now carry a green camouflage on the upper surfaces. The rudder on the MiG-21MF has been removed; the canopy, air intake and nozzle are covered by protective material. It is likely that in the event of a conflict in Europe the giant Mi-6, alongside the Mi-26, would be used to recover damaged aircraft and to carry them away from the front line to a repair shop. Such exercises were practised by the Americans in the Vietnam War.

▼68

68. A ground crew member assisting the pilot before his mission. This MiG-21MF is parked in a sheltered hangar, which gives protection to everything except a direct hit by a bomb. Most of the airfields in Eastern Europe have such shelters. The KM-1 seat used by the MiG-21MF variant is also used in the MiG-23/27 'Flogger' and the MiG-25 'Foxbat'.

69. Two MiG-21s at the Kabul Flight Academy in Afghanistan. Even after the withdrawal of Soviet troops, the 'Fishbeds' fly daily missions against the rebels. The national marking in this style was introduced for the first time in 1982. The aircraft on the left is a MiG-21MF, 'Red 324', which is painted green and sand on the upper surfaces and light blue on the undersurfaces. The 'Fishbed' on the right is a silver MiG-21PFM, 'Red 352'. The nosewheel of this aircraft is missing and the aircraft is jacked up on its nose. [*W. Łuczak*]

70. An East German MiG-21MF jacked up and undergoing a routine check. The calibration device for the 'Jay Bird' radar has been removed from the air intake. As usual to confuse Western enthusiasts, the '1' has been placed in front of the true tactical number 'Red 513'. The ground crew's overalls are black, the colour of the mechanic's dress in the wartime Luftwaffe. This picture was taken in August 1984 at Preschen, the base of Jagdfliegergeschwader 3 'Wladimir Komarow'. This unit is now converting from the MiG-21 to the MiG-29 'Fulcrum', the first unit in the East German Air Force to do so.

71. Two pilots return from a mission in their MiG-21MFs. They are wearing the VKK-6

flying suit with no helmet, but a soft cap and oxygen mask. Poland has the second largest air force in WarPac with more than 350 'Fishbeds' in current use with air force and navy units. They are painted silver or light grey and some serve in regiments on the Baltic coast where they are painted white overall.

▲72

72. Take-off of three Czech MiG-21MFs. The two aircraft nearest the camera, 'Black 5581' and 'Black 5603', are painted light grey overall, while 'Black 4401' is still in its natural metal. The SOD transponder aerial on '4401' is also silver, but bright olive green on the light-grey 'Fishbed'. The Czech Air Force MiG-21s are based at Mosnov (one regiment), Bechyne (one squadron),

Plzen (one squadron) and Zatec (one squadron).

73. MiG-21bis 'Blue 27' of a Soviet frontal fighter regiment. This aircraft is camouflaged in the Asian paint scheme. A feature of the MiG-21bis is the extended dorsal spine which reaches further into the tail fin than that of the MiG-21MF. The MiG-21bis has a large tank in the dorsal

spine and a fuel capacity of 2,900 litres. The use of titanium parts instead of steel and steel-alloy reduced the weight of the last production variant of the 'Fishbed' significantly. These aircraft of the last generation have their national markings applied on top of the wing. The red star is outlined in white with a thin red outer stripe.

▼73

74. A MiG-21bis rolls on a rainy apron to the runway. This particular machine carries the Asian camouflage of green, light grey and sand upper surfaces and light blue undersurfaces. In the Soviet regiments camouflage schemes vary sharply from one aircraft to another, in contrast to USAF practice.

75. East German MiG-21U 'Black 275' with no load carried on the pylons. The first MiG-21Us were received by the East German Air Force in early 1965, about two and a half years after the first MiG-21F-13 fighter had been supplied to the German Democratic Republic. The trainer variant of the MiG-21 lacked internal armament, but the trainer (NATO ASCC name 'Mongol') can carry the same external weapons as the fighter.

74▲ 75▼

▲76

76. MiG-21U 'Black 4916' equipped with a K-13A missile rail. The nose section was of new construction to accommodate a second seat. MiG-21 trainers were built in two plants at Moscow and Tbilisi, but there was no external difference between aircraft built by these plants.

77. Polish MiG-21U 'Red

▼77

2720' is prepared for another mission. The ground crew man is removing the steps, but the coverings on the intake relief plates on the wing root are still in place. This is the second generation of MiG-21U (version 66-600), which differs from the first variant (66-400) in having the enlarged tail fin without the fillet. The brake

chute has been moved from its compartment on the port side of the tail to the base of the rudder. [*Lech Ziela-skowski*]

78. Pilot and instructor in the cockpit of a MiG-21U. Both are wearing the VKK-4 flight combination. The MiG-21U and MiG-21US here still had the initial SK-1 ejection seat.

There is a thick glass panel between the pupil's and instructor's compartments and both have separate pressurization systems. A feature not often seen on MiG-21 trainers is the camera gun fitted above the port wing pylon. The same type of camera is used on the MiG-27 'Flogger-D'.

78▶

▲79 ▼80

79. MiG-21UM of the Magyar Legierö (Hungarian Air Force). Hungary has relatively few MiG-21UMs since the training of her pilots is done in either Czechoslovakia or the Soviet Union. The camouflage is olive drab and brown earth on upper surfaces and light blue undersurfaces. The four-digit red tactical number '3041' is outlined in white. There are currently three units equipped with the MiG-21: one squadron of the 'Stromfeld' Regiment at Pápa, two squadrons of the 'Szentgörgyi' Unit at Kecskemet and a further two squadrons of the 'Kapos' Regiment at Taszar.

80. Nose view of a MiG-21UM trainer. The small diameter of the air intake and pitot boom offset to starboard, as well only two wing pylons, are typical for the MiG-21UM. For comparison, the MiG-21F-13 has the same nose diameter, but the pitot boom is placed at the bottom of the nose. The MiG-21PF/PFM has the pitot boom placed on the centre-line on top, and a larger-diameter nose. The MiG-21MF has the pitot boom offset to starboard, but has four pylons instead of

the two on the MiG-21UM 'Mongol'.

81. Two East German MiG-21UMs on take-off. Both aircraft, 'Black 233' and 'Black 221', have olive drab and brown earth camouflage on their upper surfaces and light blue undersurfaces. However, the camouflage is quite worn on the aircraft nearest the camera. Both machines took part in Exercise 'Soyuz 81' in March and April 1981. While East German 'Fishbeds' assigned to combat units use, without exception, three-digit red tactical numbers, training aircraft only use three-digit black numbers. There are some trainers assigned to each of the five fighter regiments equipped with the 'Fishbed', but the bulk is allocated to the Jagdflieger-ausbildungsgeschwader 25 (Fighter Pilot Training Unit/Advanced Training Unit 25) 'Leander Ratz', which is based at Rothenburg, near the Polish border in the south of the German Democratic Republic.

81▲

82. Czech MiG-21UM 'Black 1061' departs for a training sortie with the instructor's periscope fully extended. The instructor's view is rather limited since his seat is level with that of the pupil. Similar to the MiG-21PFM, the MiG-21UM is equipped with SPS blown flaps.

82▼

▲83

83. Instructor and pupil check an East German MiG-21UM, 'Black 262', prior to a training sortie. This aircraft belongs to Jagdfliegergeschwader 1 'Fritz Schmenkel' based at Holzdorf. The 'Fritz Schmenkel Regiment' was previously based at Cottbus, but this is now home base to

▼84

the Kampfhubschraubergeschwader 67 'Ferdinand von Schill' equipped with Mi-8TBK and Mi-24 'Hind-D' helicopters. Similar to the third-generation MiG-21MF, the MiG-21UM was also equipped with the angle of attack transmitter on the port side of the nose.

84. MiG-21MF 'Red 6514' of the Polish Air Force adorned with a badge of a lynx's head on a playing card on the nose above the angle of attack transmitter. The aircraft is painted light grey overall. The Polish Air Force has a badge for almost each squadron but they are

seldom carried on aircraft. The playing card as an emblem was quite popular in the German and Italian Air Forces during the Second World War. This particular MiG-21MF is carrying UB-16-57U pods on the inboard wing pylon. [*Wojtek Łuczak*]

85. This MiG-21bis belongs to the Afghan Military Flying Academy at Kabul. It is finished in Asian camouflage brown-sand-olive drab on the upper surfaces and light blue on the under surfaces. The tyres are painted white to reflect the sun better than black does. The MiG-21MFs still see considerable action in combat despite the Soviet withdrawal. Several pilots flew no less than three missions each day against the rebels. This type of national marking was introduced in 1982 and replaced the early Afghan marking of a red dot with yellow inscription. [*Wojtek Łuczak*]

86. An Afghan Air Force MiG-21UM trainer at Kabul in 1987. The smaller nose diameter clearly denotes a MiG-21 trainer, even when the canopy has been covered by a canvas to protect it from the sun. This aircraft is painted silver overall with tactical number '578' in red. The tail rotor in the background belongs to a Mi-8TB 'Hip-C' helicopter. This particular MiG-21UM is equipped with a missile rail; however the MiG-21UMs are rarely used in combat against the rebels. [*Wojtek Łuczak*]

87. Mongolian pilots who are trained by Soviet instructors. The insignia on the tail is red, as are the three digit tactical numbers not visible here. The Mongolians only have twelve MiG-21s so this photograph shows half their MiG-21 pilots.

85▲ 86▼

87▼

88. A Cuban MiG-21PFM undergoing pre-mission checks. The Fuerza Aerea Revolutionaria is currently replacing its six squadrons of 120 'Fishbeds' with the MiG-29 'Fulcrum', operational in Cuba since April 1990.

▲88 ▼89

89. North Vietnamese pilots ready and waiting at an air base near Hanoi to take off on interceptor missions against intruding American aircraft. Most NVAF aircraft carried four-digit tactical numbers in red. Today, the NVAF has about 150 MiG-21s of various types.